My Parenting Journey

with an LGBTQ+ Child

A Journal

My Parenting Journey

with an LGBTQ+ Child

A Journal

by

Cheryl B. Evans

Published by Cheryl B. Evans - Ontario, Canada

www.writtenbymom.ca

You are encouraged to have fun with your journal.
Write, draw and create your own magic within its pages.

First Published in 2018

Paperback ISBN: 978-1-7753526-0-0

First Edition

Throughout this book (and in the title) you will notice the + symbol after
LGBTQ. The author has used this symbol to ensure no child is overlooked.
All our children have the right to self-identity however they choose and
the + symbol is a way to ensure no child is left out.

Library and Archives Canada Cataloguing in Publication

Printed in the United States of America

Other books by Cheryl B. Evans include:
I Promised Not to Tell: Raising a transgender child
What Does God Think? Transgender People and The Bible
Wonderfully and Purposely Made: I Am Enough – A Journal All About Me
My Parenting Journey with a Transgender Child – A Journal

My Parenting Journey

with an LGBTQ+ Child

A Journal

My Parenting Journey

with an LGBTQ+ Child

This journal was created to help you to process, understand, and grow through your unique experience of raising an LGBTQ+ child. So, go ahead - splash your style, charisma, and individuality across the pages, and don't forget to share a little of your heart and soul along the way.

The Date I started this journal: / /

Doodle, write, and create magic within these pages to your heart's content.

Introduction

As you may already know, I am the mother of a transgender child. The journey our family took toward discovering our daughter was actually our son was not an easy one. There were many ups and downs and a ton of new information to learn, process, and acknowledge. Today, parents of LGBTQ+ kids have access to far more information than we had when Jordan came out to us. However, easier access to information doesn't mean you don't still experience a rollercoaster of emotions.

One of the greatest gifts I gave myself after Jordan first came out to my husband, Jim, and I was the gift of journaling. It was my own private time. I wrote about how I was coping, how my transgender child was coping, and how each member of our family was affected by the changes we were experiencing. Journaling helped me to process everything. It was an opportunity to document important milestones, dates, and events related to my son coming out as a transgender teen. Journaling was my outlet and my saving grace some days. I honestly believe journaling helped me to be a better parent as we waded through unchartered waters.

After seeing firsthand how truly therapeutic journaling can be, I wanted to create something to help other parents who are walking a similar path. In addition to writing, colouring can also be therapeutic and relaxing. For this reason, you will find a few whimsical images placed throughout your journal.

My previously published memoir, titled *I Promised Not to Tell*, was born out of my own journaling, and although I believe that publishing our family's story has helped, it wasn't enough. Reading a story that you can relate to can be comforting and even reassuring. However, when you journal about your own parenting journey, the depth of your experience can be so much greater.

There are many journals on the market today, but none specifically designed for parents of LGBTQ+ kids - until now. *My Parenting Journey with an LGBTQ+ Child* was created just for you. It is my hope that through the various writing prompts, activities, and information in this journal, you, too, will experience something wonderful. Who knows? You may even decide to write your own book one day, and this journal could be just the tool you need to help you do that. Parenting is a journey full of surprises, but when you are the parent of an LGBTQ+ child, life gets a whole lot more interesting.

I hope this journal enhances your personal journey in a positive way.

My sincere blessings to you and your family,

Cheryl B. Evans

Chapter

One

The Parent in Me

My Child is Wonderfully
and Purposely Made.

My Parenting Journey

with an LGBTQ+ Child

My name:

_____

My child's name(s):

_____

Parenting an LGBTQ+ child can be an extraordinary journey. My personal parenting experiences are as unique and individual as I am and my child is. Here is what being a parent of an LGBTQ+ child means to me:

_____
_____
_____
_____
_____
_____
_____
_____
_____
_____
_____

I first knew my child was LGBTQ+ when…

_____

_____

_____

_____

_____

What I remember about that day or time is…

_____

_____

_____

_____

_____

_____

_____

_____

_____

I remember feeling…

_____

_____

_____

_____

_____

The person I first shared my child's truth with was:

_____

Their reaction to this truth was...

_____

_____

_____

_____

_____

_____

Looking back, I can honestly say...

_____

_____

_____

_____

_____

_____

_____

_____

_____

_____

_____

_____

Through my LGBTQ+ child's eyes, I think they see me as a parent who...

_____

_____

_____

_____

_____

_____

_____

_____

How does the way I believe my child sees me affect me as a parent?

_____

_____

_____

_____

_____

_____

_____

_____

_____

_____

_____

What do I wish my LGBTQ+ child could understand about me in regard to their coming out?

If I had the opportunity to change something about the way I reacted when my child came out to me, would I take it? If so, what would I change? If not, why?

_____

_____

_____

_____

_____

_____

_____

_____

_____

_____

_____

_____

_____

_____

_____

_____

_____

_____

_____

My Parenting Style

I define my parenting style as…

_____

_____

_____

_____

_____

_____

_____

_____

_____

Does it differ from my spouse's, partner's, or ex's parenting style?

_____

_____

_____

_____

_____

_____

How have our different or similar parenting styles impacted the parenting of my LGBTQ+ child?

What is a challenging parenting moment I've experienced since my child came out to me?

What are some of my best parenting qualities?

_____
_____
_____
_____
_____
_____
_____
_____

How have these qualities helped me in parenting my LGBTQ+ child?

_____
_____
_____
_____
_____
_____
_____
_____
_____
_____
_____
_____
_____

This was the process I went through in acknowledging and accepting my LGBTQ+ child:

_____

_____

_____

_____

_____

_____

_____

_____

_____

_____

_____

_____

_____

_____

_____

_____

_____

_____

_____

_____

_____

_____

_____

_____

_____

What, if any, were my biggest misconceptions about parents of LGBTQ+ kids before my child came out?

_____

_____

_____

_____

_____

_____

_____

_____

_____

_____

What, if any, were my biggest misconceptions about LGBTQ+ kids before my child came out?

_____

_____

_____

_____

_____

_____

_____

_____

Sometimes even affirming parents have a hard time accepting or dealing with certain aspects of having an LGBTQ+ child. Something that I still struggle with is...

_____

_____

_____

_____

_____

_____

_____

_____

_____

_____

_____

_____

_____

_____

_____

_____

_____

_____

_____

_____

_____

It's common for parents of LGBTQ+ kids to have regrets about how they reacted or even how they felt when their child came out – this is perfectly normal. What, if any, are some of the regrets I have?

Shame is another common emotion that parents of LGBTQ+ kids experience. How have I experienced shame or been shamed by others?

_____

_____

_____

_____

_____

_____

_____

_____

_____

_____

_____

_____

_____

_____

_____

_____

_____

_____

_____

Parents of LGBTQ+ kids, particularly parents of transgender kids, often say they had to mourn the loss of the child as they knew them. Time often reveals to us that it was our expectations, not the child, we had to mourn. As common as these encounters are, they can still be heart-wrenching to experience. What are the feelings of mourning I've had or am having for my child or my vision for their life?

What other emotions have I felt since my child came out?

Sometimes we will
never know the
value of a moment
until it becomes a
memory.

Dr. Seuss

A special parenting moment I'd like to document so I don't forget is...

_____

_____

_____

_____

_____

_____

_____

_____

_____

_____

_____

_____

_____

_____

_____

_____

_____

_____

_____

_____

_____

_____

Write about the first time I met another parent with a LGBTQ+ child.

If that hasn't happened yet, how would I imagine the experience to be?

Some of the ways I've grown through my unique parenting experiences are…

_____

_____

_____

_____

_____

_____

_____

_____

_____

_____

_____

_____

_____

_____

_____

_____

_____

_____

_____

_____

_____

_____

Here's a letter to my future self with some awesome parenting advice... (Don't forget to date it. ☺)

Chapter

Two

My LGBTQ+ Child

My LGBTQ+ Child

The things I love about my LGBTQ+ child are...

_____

_____

_____

_____

_____

_____

_____

_____

What has my LGBTQ+ child taught me?

_____

_____

_____

_____

_____

_____

_____

_____

How does my LGBTQ+ child identify, and how has it changed our relationship from before they came out (if, in fact, our relationship has changed)?

Not Everyone Gets Us, And That is OK!

The harsh reality is that many people just don't understand the parenting journey of having a LGBTQ+ child. Many people don't even try to understand. How do you choose to respond to others who are not supportive or affirming?

My kind and patient version...

_____

_____

_____

_____

_____

_____

_____

_____

_____

_____

_____

_____

_____

_____

Now, my brutally honest, in-your-face version...

_____

_____

_____

_____

_____

_____

_____

_____

_____

_____

_____

_____

_____

_____

_____

_____

_____

_____

_____

That felt good!

Prickly situations – we all have them. Sometimes it's the people closest to us that can hurt us the most.

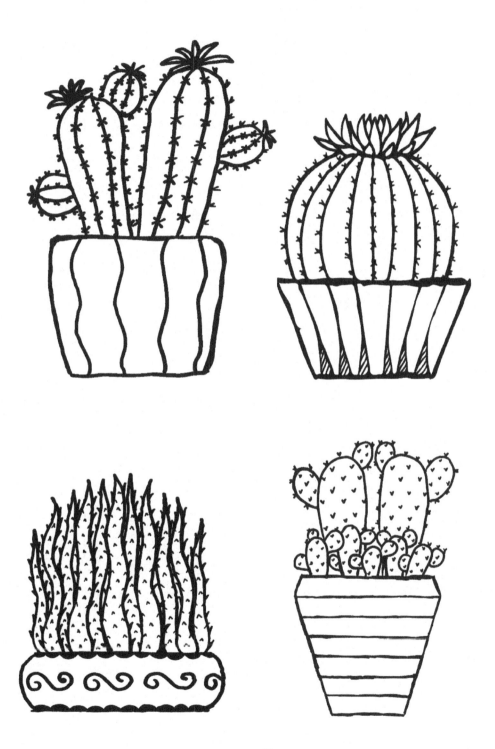

There may be people whom we need to keep at arms length for the sake of our LGBTQ+ kids. This doesn't mean it is easy pushing them away. Who are those people for me, and how has keeping them at a distance affected me emotionally?

Before my LGBTQ+ child came out to me, what were my thoughts on the LGBTQ+ community?

_____
_____
_____
_____
_____
_____
_____
_____
_____
_____

How have my feelings changed since my child came out as LGBTQ+?

_____
_____
_____
_____
_____
_____
_____
_____
_____

What are some of the things I have done to shelter my LGBTQ+ child?

_____

_____

_____

_____

_____

_____

_____

_____

_____

_____

_____

What do I think would have happened if I hadn't sheltered them?

_____

_____

_____

_____

_____

_____

_____

Who is someone who was unable or unwilling to accept my LGBTQ+ child? Why has it been an issue for them, and how has their reaction affected me and my family?

What do these challenges teach me about myself?

Write about a time you and your child bonded after
they came out and what that time meant to you.

There Will Be Tears and That's OK!

Write about a time I allowed negative tears to flow. Maybe I was scared or sad. What was happening, and what was going through my mind at the time?

_____

_____

_____

_____

_____

_____

_____

_____

_____

_____

_____

_____

_____

_____

_____

_____

_____

_____

_____

_____

_____

_____

Write about a time I shed tears of joy.

Sometimes it can feel as if we are on an emotional rollercoaster. How have the highs and lows affected me, and what have I learned from them?

_____

_____

_____

_____

_____

_____

_____

_____

_____

_____

_____

_____

_____

_____

_____

_____

_____

_____

_____

_____

_____

_____

_____

Sometimes LGBTQ+ people don't like looking at photos of themselves before they came out. Are there times I've had to put away photos or sentimental things that my child doesn't want to see? How have I felt about this?

We all need to let off steam from time to time. This page is for me to vent about anyone that has caused me worry or stress simply by their reaction or opinion of my child being LGBTQ+.

Okay, seriously – I'm going to need another page for that. I've got more to say about the reaction of others...

Remember to breathe.

You got this!

Chapter
Three

Gratitude

Start each
day with a
grateful

Gratitude

The feeling of being grateful and giving thanks for what we already have is one of the most powerful practices we can use for a positive and joyous life.

Gratitude Challenge: Every day, for the next 100 days, write something I am grateful for.

1. _____
2. _____
3. _____
4. _____
5. _____
6. _____
7. _____
8. _____
9. _____
10. _____
11. _____
12. _____
13. _____
14. _____
15. _____
16. _____
17. _____
18. _____
19. _____
20. _____
21. _____

22. _____

23. _____

24. _____

25. _____

26. _____

27. _____

28. _____

29. _____

30. _____

31. _____

32. _____

33. _____

34. _____

35. _____

36. _____

37. _____

38. _____

39. _____

40. _____

41. _____

42. _____

43. _____

44. _____

45. _____

46. _____

47. _____

48. _____

49. _____

50. _____

51. _____

52. _____

53. _____

54. _____

55. _____

56. _____

57. _____

58. _____

59. _____

60. _____

61. _____

62. _____

63. _____

64. _____

65. _____

66. _____

67. _____

68. _____

69. _____

70. _____

71. _____

72. _____

73. _____

74. _____

75. _____

76. _____

77. _____

78. _____

79. _____

80. _____

81. _____

82. _____

83. _____

84. _____

85. _____

86. _____

87. _____

88. _____

89. _____

90. _____

91. _____

92. _____

93. _____

94. _____

95. _____

96. _____

97. _____

98. _____

99. _____

100. _____

 Whenever I need to add a little thankfulness to my day, this list will serve as a reminder that there is ALWAYS someone, someplace, or something to be grateful for.

The People I am Grateful For and Why:

I am truly grateful when others:

The Places I am Grateful For and Why:

_____

_____

_____

_____

_____

_____

_____

_____

_____

_____

_____

_____

_____

_____

_____

_____

_____

_____

_____

_____

_____

_____

_____

The Things I am Grateful For and Why:

A thank you note to someone I owe a debt of gratitude to:

Chapter

Four

Happiness & Joy

Sometimes our LGBTQ+ children can be
unhappy or depressed, and it's heartbreaking
for us, as parents, to witness this.

Often, there are things going on with our
children that we know little about. They
don't always share their deepest thoughts
with us, and this can leave us feeling frustrated,
apprehensive, and even scared.

As parents of LGBTQ+ children, we can
strive to do our best, though it's important
to acknowledge we can't control the happiness or
inner joy of another person, not even our own child's.

What we can do is positively contribute to the happiness of our LGBTQ+ children. We can do that by serving up unconditional love.

And maybe a cupcake or two ☺

Happiness ☺

These are some of the things that make me happy:

_____

_____

_____

_____

_____

_____

_____

_____

_____

_____

_____

_____

_____

_____

_____

_____

_____

_____

My happy 'peeps' are those who make me smile. They lift me up and make me laugh. They are the deliverers of my sunshine. They are the friends I can always count on. Here's a little about them and how they have helped me on my parenting journey:

Parenting is busy work, and every now and again, the need to escape strikes me. When it does, what do I do and where do I go?

My Greatest Joy

When or where do I experience my greatest joy? Is it when I am alone in nature? Listening to music? Singing in the shower? Here are my experiences:

Some of my thoughts on a new skill or hobby that I would like to pursue just for the joy of it:

_____

_____

_____

_____

_____

_____

_____

_____

_____

Where could I go to find out more about that?

_____

_____

_____

_____

_____

_____

_____

_____

My child's innate gender and/or sexual identity is one to be celebrated, protected, and cherished. What, if anything, is blocking my ability to celebrate my child's diversity?

_____

_____

_____

_____

_____

_____

_____

_____

_____

_____

_____

_____

_____

_____

_____

_____

_____

_____

_____

How can I celebrate my uniqueness as a parent of an LGBTQ+ child and find more joy in my life?

As a parent, I need to remember to take care of me. What are some ways I can do that?

_____

_____

_____

_____

_____

_____

_____

_____

_____

_____

_____

_____

_____

_____

_____

_____

_____

_____

_____

_____

_____

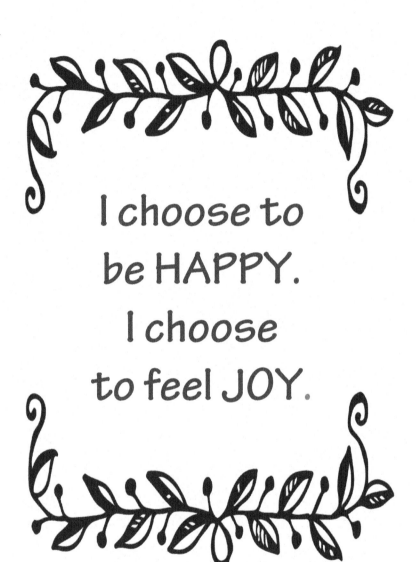

I choose to
be HAPPY.
I choose
to feel JOY.

In what ways does my LGBTQ+ child bring me joy?

_____
_____
_____
_____
_____
_____
_____
_____
_____
_____

What can I do to help elevate the happiness of my LGBTQ+ child?

_____
_____
_____
_____
_____
_____
_____
_____
_____

Life is Richer with Books

This is a list of some of the best books I have enjoyed and some of the books I want to read.

Books I Enjoyed:

_____
_____
_____
_____
_____
_____
_____
_____
_____
_____

Books I Want to Read:

_____
_____
_____
_____
_____
_____
_____
_____
_____

If my life were a book, the title would be:

_____

This is the first paragraph of my story:

_____
_____
_____
_____
_____
_____
_____
_____
_____
_____
_____
_____
_____
_____
_____
_____
_____
_____
_____

It was the funniest thing...

This page is dedicated to remembering my crazy moments and silly mishaps - those times that bring a smile to my face whenever I recall them.

My Happiest Day Since My Child Came Out

When was it? What happened? Who was there?

_____

_____

_____

_____

_____

_____

_____

_____

_____

_____

_____

_____

_____

_____

_____

_____

_____

_____

Laughter is Food for the Soul.

These are things I can do today to laugh more:

_____

_____

_____

_____

_____

_____

_____

_____

_____

_____

_____

_____

_____

_____

_____

A joke or a memory that always makes me laugh:

_____

_____

_____

_____

Chapter

Five

Love & Family

Love

Love flows through my heart,
out to others, and back to me.

One of the most important things to know about love is that it starts with me. Before I can show love to others, I must first have love for myself. Self-love is something we should all strive for, but for some, it is not an easy task. What can I do to show myself more love?

_____

_____

_____

_____

_____

_____

_____

_____

_____

_____

_____

_____

_____

_____

_____

_____

_____

_____

When was a time I doubted myself as a parent? How I can encourage myself more to reduce self-doubt in the future?

_____

_____

_____

_____

_____

_____

_____

_____

_____

_____

_____

_____

_____

_____

_____

_____

_____

_____

How I speak to myself about myself
is more important than any words
anyone else can ever say to me.

What can I begin telling myself today that can help me to love and encourage myself more?

How can I show more love to others?

♡

_____

_____

_____

_____

_____

_____

_____

_____

How can others show me more love?

♡

_____

_____

_____

_____

_____

_____

_____

_____

_____

When others judge my parenting abilities or my child's authentic self, how can I respond from a place of love?

_____

_____

_____

_____

_____

_____

_____

_____

How can I adjust my own thinking to make it easier to deal with negative comments from others?

_____

_____

_____

_____

_____

_____

_____

_____

What positive things do others tell me about myself that I
sometimes have difficulty receiving?

_____

_____

_____

_____

_____

_____

_____

_____

_____

_____

_____

_____

_____

_____

How can I adjust my thinking to make accepting these compliments
easier - and make it easier to believe them?

_____

_____

_____

_____

_____

_____

The mind believes what
you tell it. Feed your
child's mind with faith,
strength, truth, and love.

Family Members

Write about a family member who had a positive and loving reaction to my child coming out as LGBTQ+.

Is there a family member who was unable or unwilling to accept my LGBTQ+ child? Who are they? Why has it been an issue for them, and how has their reaction affected me and my family?

These are a few pictures of me and my LGBTQ+ child I cherish:

(Paste or staple them below.)

These are a few pictures of me and other family members I cherish:

What could I do to let someone know I love them if I were unable to speak?

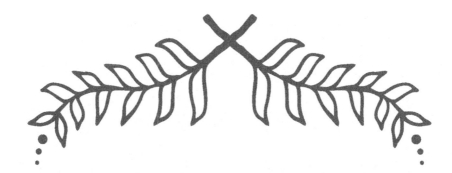

Being the parent of
an LGBTQ+ child
is about loving
beyond our own
expectations.

Who is the person I admire most in the world? Why?

Who can I always count on? What does it mean to me to have them in my life?

_____

_____

_____

_____

_____

_____

_____

_____

_____

_____

_____

_____

_____

_____

_____

_____

_____

_____

_____

_____

_____

Art from Emotion

Let's find out what my emotions look like as art.

Select a colour to represent each emotion listed below. Start by assigning a colour to the right of each emotion, creating your own colour/emotion legend.

Accomplished	Angry
Calm	Confident
Determined	Disappointed
Excited	Fearful
Happy	Joyful
Loved	Optimistic
Peaceful	Relieved
Sorrow	Surprised
Thankful	Worried

Each day, colour a space in the art on the opposite page with the colour that represents your most predominate emotion that day. Repeat until the art piece is complete.

Art is made
beautiful
with emotion.

Art Reflection

Based on the colours in my art piece, which emotion did I experience the most often?

_____

Which emotion did I experience the least?

_____

Did this surprise me? If so, why or why not?

_____
_____
_____
_____
_____
_____
_____
_____
_____
_____
_____

A Positive Life

One of the ways to live a more positive life is to convert negative thoughts or emotions into positive ones.

(Use this page to record some of your own examples.)

Chapter

Six

Dreams & Goals

What does a goal of LGBTQ+ equality look like to me?

Here's the most vivid dream I've had and what I think it means:

I Have a Dream...
A beautiful dream...

I dream…

_____

_____

_____

_____

_____

_____

_____

_____

_____

_____

_____

_____

_____

_____

_____

_____

_____

_____

_____

_____

_____

_____

If I knew I couldn't fail, what would I do?

Goals are Dreams with a Plan

Here's a list of some of my goals for the coming year:

_____

_____

_____

_____

_____

_____

_____

_____

_____

_____

_____

_____

_____

_____

_____

_____

A list of at least ten things I'd like to accomplish in my lifetime:

_____

_____

_____

_____

_____

_____

_____

_____

_____

_____

_____

_____

_____

_____

_____

_____

_____

_____

_____

_____

_____

What are the keys to successfully parenting a LGBTQ+ child I wish everyone would follow?

_____

_____

_____

_____

_____

_____

_____

_____

_____

_____

_____

_____

_____

Have my dreams for my child changed since they came out?

Chapter

Seven

Strength & Wisdom

Being Brave

As the parent, I sometimes feel fear or concern for my LGBTQ+ child. Here's my opportunity to explore that by writing about what specifically worries me the most.

_____

_____

_____

_____

_____

_____

_____

_____

_____

_____

_____

_____

_____

_____

_____

_____

_____

_____

_____

A list of the ways I stay brave and ward off fear:

The bravest person I know is _____ because...

_____
_____
_____
_____
_____
_____
_____
_____
_____
_____
_____

What can I learn from this person?

_____
_____
_____
_____
_____
_____
_____
_____
_____

Who do I look up to who is a strong ally or activist for the LGBTQ+ community, and why?

Wisdom

With each day, week, month, and year that passes, I gain wisdom.
I am already much wiser than I used to be. If I could go back between
five and ten years, what advice would I give to my younger self?

_____

_____

_____

_____

_____

_____

_____

_____

_____

_____

_____

_____

_____

_____

_____

_____

_____

_____

_____

_____

I am strong when I
understand my weaknesses.

My weaknesses are...

_____

_____

_____

_____

_____

_____

_____

_____

_____

_____

_____

_____

_____

_____

_____

_____

_____

_____

_____

_____

_____

_____

I remember a difficult time in my life when...

How did I handle that difficult situation? If I could go back in time, what, if anything, would I do differently?

Good parents
listen more than
they speak.
Great parents
love beyond words.

The Not-So-Bright Spots
and what they've taught me...

Sometimes life sucks, but there's usually a lesson in there somewhere. What lessons have I learned from the not-so-bright times in my life or my child's life?

Remember a time I fought for something I believed in. How did that experience make me feel?

If someone younger than myself was looking to me for wisdom, what life lessons would I share with them?

(lined writing space)

When we are wise, we recognize that some people are good for us, and others are not.

Who should I be spending more time with? Why?

_____
_____
_____
_____
_____
_____
_____
_____
_____

Who should I be spending less time with? Why?

_____
_____
_____
_____
_____
_____
_____

Keeping a Healthy Mind

A negative mind will never give me a positive life.
We can only attain what our mind believes we can attain.
Changing my mind can change my life.

What do I believe about myself as a parent today?

_____

_____

_____

_____

_____

_____

_____

_____

_____

_____

_____

_____

_____

_____

_____

_____

I'm not average. I'm awesome!

Improving My Mind, Body, and Soul

What could I work on that would help me improve my overall health?

_____

_____

_____

_____

_____

_____

_____

_____

_____

_____

What positive things do I already do that help me maintain good health?

_____

_____

_____

_____

_____

_____

_____

My Go-to List
Help and inspiration when needed

Friends I can call on:

_____

_____

_____

_____

_____

_____

Websites:

_____

_____

_____

_____

_____

_____

_____

Help Lines:

_____

_____

_____

_____

_____

Places to go for inspiration:

Other important resources:

After My Child Came Out:

Memories of Important Milestones

_____

_____

_____

_____

_____

_____

_____

_____

_____

_____

_____

_____

_____

_____

_____

_____

_____

_____

_____

_____

_____

_____

_____

Extra Notes

Chapter

Eight

More Great Stuff

Fun Facts:

It was on purpose that there are eight chapters in this journal.

Spiritually, the number eight is a personal power number that
represents inner wisdom, self-confidence, and truth.
It represents a life path with balance, harmony,
strength, and meaning.

The number eight has no beginning and no end. On its side, it
is the mathematical symbol for infinity. It represents
endless abundance in love, supply, time, and energy.

The number eight is also the atomic number for oxygen,
which is pretty important to us as humans.

There are many twists and turns in life.

Your individual experiences, planned or not, make you who you are. The more you experience the twists and turns in life, the richer your life will be.

Here are some of the more memorable twists and turns I've experienced since my child came out as LGBTQ+...

_____

_____

_____

_____

_____

_____

_____

_____

_____

_____

_____

_____

_____

_____

_____

_____

_____

_____

_____

_____

_____

_____

_____

_____

_____

_____

What are the best things about living in the world today?

What are the worst things about living in the world today?

One person can make a difference.

What can I do to make the world a better place?

_____

_____

_____

_____

_____

_____

_____

_____

_____

_____

_____

_____

_____

_____

_____

_____

_____

_____

_____

_____

_____

_____

A list of the things I should try to do more often:

_____

_____

_____

_____

_____

_____

_____

_____

_____

_____

_____

_____

_____

_____

_____

_____

_____

_____

_____

_____

_____

_____

_____

_____

A little about my favourite movies or TV shows that feature a
LGBTQ+ person and why I like them:

_____
_____
_____
_____
_____
_____
_____
_____
_____
_____
_____
_____
_____
_____
_____
_____
_____
_____

If I could sit on a bench and talk for an hour with anyone, past or present, who would it be? What would I want to talk about?

_____

_____

_____

_____

_____

_____

_____

_____

_____

_____

_____

_____

_____

_____

_____

_____

_____

_____

_____

_____

_____

_____

Life is An Adventure

Life may not always turn out the way we expect, but
that doesn't mean the journey you are on is
not the one you were meant to take.

What if we are all spiritual beings here to learn
from what this world can teach us? In the school
of life, there are no wrong lessons. Sure, some are
tougher than others to master, and some are near
impossible, but each lesson is invaluable. You succeed in
life not when you master everything, but when you decide
to try, to step up and be the best person you can be
in the time you are here.

Remember to rejoice in life because even in the most
trying times, you are learning, growing, and expanding
as the unique and wonderful being that you are.

Enjoy the Journey!

Fun Facts:

The first rainbow flag was created as a symbol of pride and hope for the LGBT (lesbian, gay, bisexual and transgender) community in 1978. It was designed and stitched together by Gilbert Baker Designs. Harvey Milk is credited for providing the inspiration. Thirty-one years later, then President Barack Obama awarded the highest civilian honour, the Medal of Freedom, posthumously to Harvey Milk.

The first documented gay rights organization was founded by Henry Gerber out of Chicago in 1924. That organization is The Society for Human Rights.

The Advocate is considered the oldest continuing LGBT publication with fifty-plus years to its credit. It was originally founded by Personal Rights in Defense and Education (PRIDE) in 1967 as a newsletter published under the name *The Los Angeles Advocate*. It was renamed *The Advocate* two years later.

Pride Month is officially celebrated in the month of June each year. This well-known event originated from a riot that took place back in June of 1969. At that time, it was illegal for LGBT people to meet in public. One June evening, as police attempted to raid a bar full of LGBT people, they fought back. They decided they would not be removed. For the next few days, LGBT people took to the streets, and it was then that PRIDE was born.

We can't always protect our children but we can be there for them when they need us. What are some of the ways I can be there for my child?

Final Notes & Other Random Stuff:

This journal may be complete, but your story is not. Keep journaling and recording all the experiences and lessons life offers you. One day, you may decide to share your story with the world, and this journal can serve as a piece of your history to help you do just that.

I Finished This Journal:

/ /

Made in the USA
Monee, IL
27 January 2020